For Kevin Rice & Tracy Burgess
"Spirits travel without limits." –Keith Haring

–Matthew Burgess

In memory of 趙芸.

–Josh Cochran

"In a way it's as important to communicate to one person, to one ten-year-old person that's growing up, as it is to try to make any big effect on the entire world."

—Keith Haring

"He's there painting on walls and running around the world, and kids flock to watch him do it... The intensity — the way he approaches a wall — with total openness, is the way he approaches *you*! [Keith] is, in the best sense of the word, childlike — open."

—Timothy Leary

www.enchantedlion.com

First published in 2020 by
Enchanted Lion Books, 248 Creamer Street, Studio 4, Brooklyn, NY 11231
Text Copyright © 2020 by Matthew Burgess
Illustration Copyright © 2020 by Josh Cochran
Book design by Josh Cochran and Sarah Klinger
All rights reserved under International and Pan-American Copyright Conventions
A CIP is on record with the Library of Congress
ISBN 978-1-59270-2671

Printed in China by R. R. Donnelley Asia Printing Solutions, Ltd.
Third Printing

DRAWING ON WALLS

A STORY OF KEITH HARING

BY MATTHEW BURGESS

PICTURES BY JOSH COCHRAN

Enchanted Lion Books
NEW YORK

Here is Keith Haring painting a mural with hundreds of children in Tama City, Japan.

Keith draws the outlines and the kids fill them in with their own designs.

When Keith was a kid, he and his dad often drew together.

They took turns making lines and watched as a balloon became an ice cream cone, or a dog transformed into a fire-breathing dragon!

Sometimes they even drew with their eyes closed.

Keith drew all the time, everywhere.

"But not on the walls!" his mother would call,
just as he was getting some big ideas.

Keith was the oldest in his family, and gradually, as he grew, three sisters arrived. First Kay, then Karen, and finally, when Keith was twelve, Kristen was born. They lived in Kutztown, a small town in Pennsylvania.

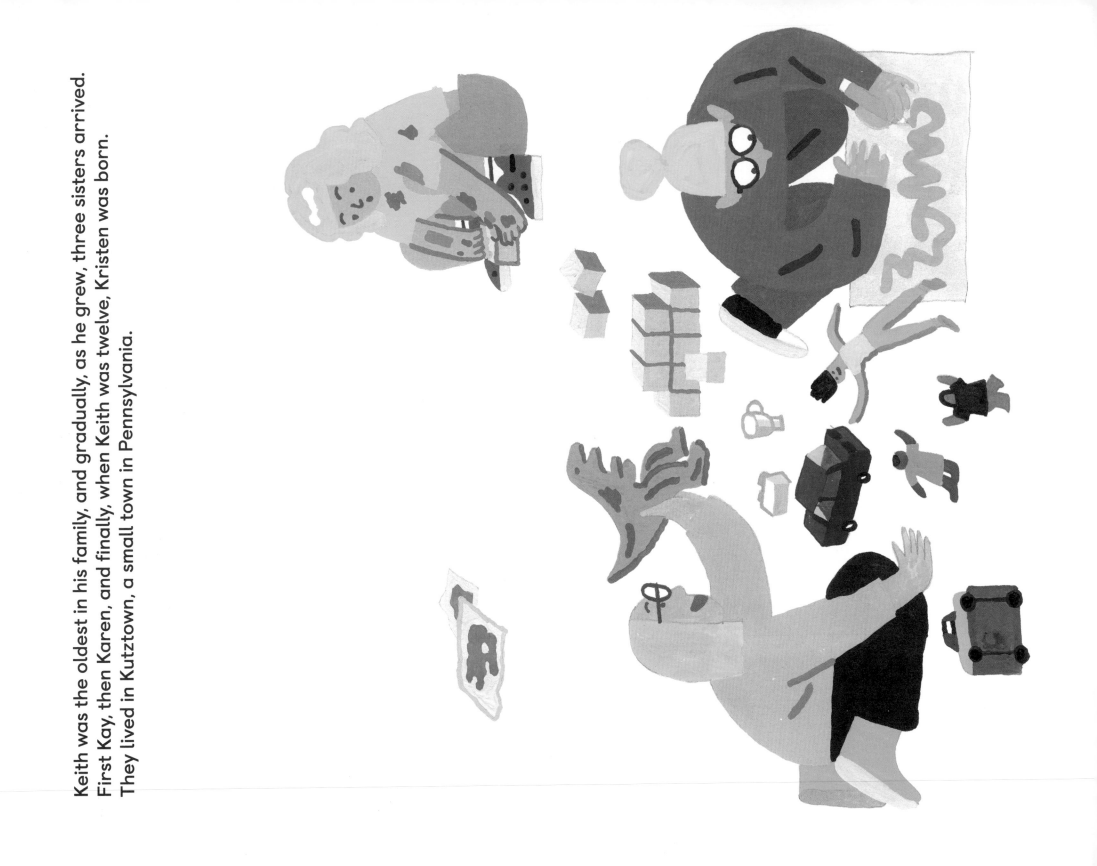

Keith loved being a big brother.

In the summer, he organized games and carnival contests in the backyard, and he would invite the entire neighborhood.

He also formed clubs with secret passwords and made little houses where friends would play.

When Kristen was old enough to hold a crayon, Keith invented a game like one his dad had taught him.

Each would draw on a sheet of paper and when someone shouted "STOP!" they'd swap sheets and continue drawing.

Keith also painted Kristen's hands and pressed them on paper to make prints.

Look — a mobile!

Keith's best friend, Kermit, loved making things too.
At school, they were known as "The Artists."

Eager to have a studio all their own, they cleared
some space in Kermit's aunt's garage.

Keith loved drawing anything with a twisting,
turning line...

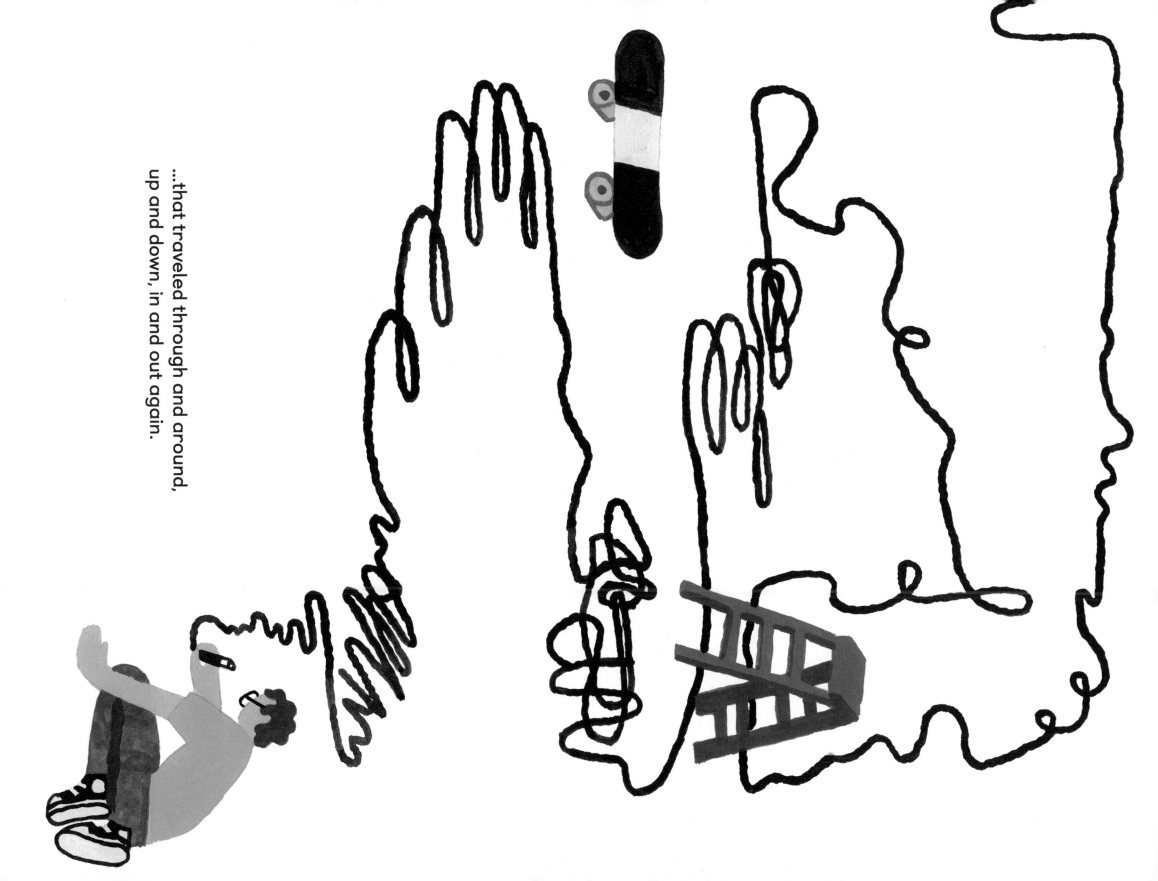

...that traveled through and around, up and down, in and out again.

When Keith was 16, he began to feel restless in Kutztown.

That summer, he caught a bus to Ocean City, New Jersey, where he lived a block from the beach with kids from Pittsburgh and New York City.

Keith washed dishes to pay his way, and in his free time, he drew. Sometimes he would stay up all night and watch the sunrise.

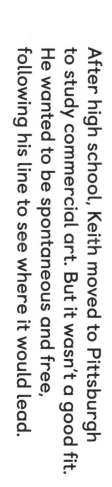

After high school, Keith moved to Pittsburgh to study commercial art. But it wasn't a good fit. He wanted to be spontaneous and free, following his line to see where it would lead.

On a trip home for Christmas, Keith stumbled upon *The Art Spirit* by Robert Henri.

After a few sentences, he felt as if the book was speaking directly to him, like a friend.

"Do whatever you do intensely. The artist... leaves the crowd and goes pioneering."

Art will never leave me and never should.

The music, dance, and visual arts, the forms of expression, the arts of hope. This is where I think I fit in...

So Keith left school, took several jobs, and saved enough money to hitchhike across the country.

He was searching for his next big step and he took *The Art Spirit* with him.

When Keith returned to Pittsburgh,
he spent hours in the library
reading about artists he admired.

He also saw an exhibition of enormous
paintings by Pierre Alechinsky.

Keith was blown away!

Inspired, Keith now knew what he had to do to find the intensity and freedom that he desired.

Keith arrived in New York City
and enrolled at the School of Visual Arts.

He was 20 years old.

One day, he found rolls of paper
that someone had tossed into the gutter.

He unrolled them in the studio at school
and began making bigger and bigger paintings.

Keith especially liked painting on the floor by the open door where the sunlight poured in.

People passing on the street would stop to watch or talk with him about what he was making. Keith loved it!

He didn't believe that some people understand art while others don't — or that art should be hidden away in galleries, museums, and private collections.

Keith wanted to communicate with as many people as possible. "The public has a right to art... Art is for everybody."

The East Village was Keith's new neighborhood.

With his friends he formed Club 57, a local hangout in the basement of a church on St. Mark's Place.

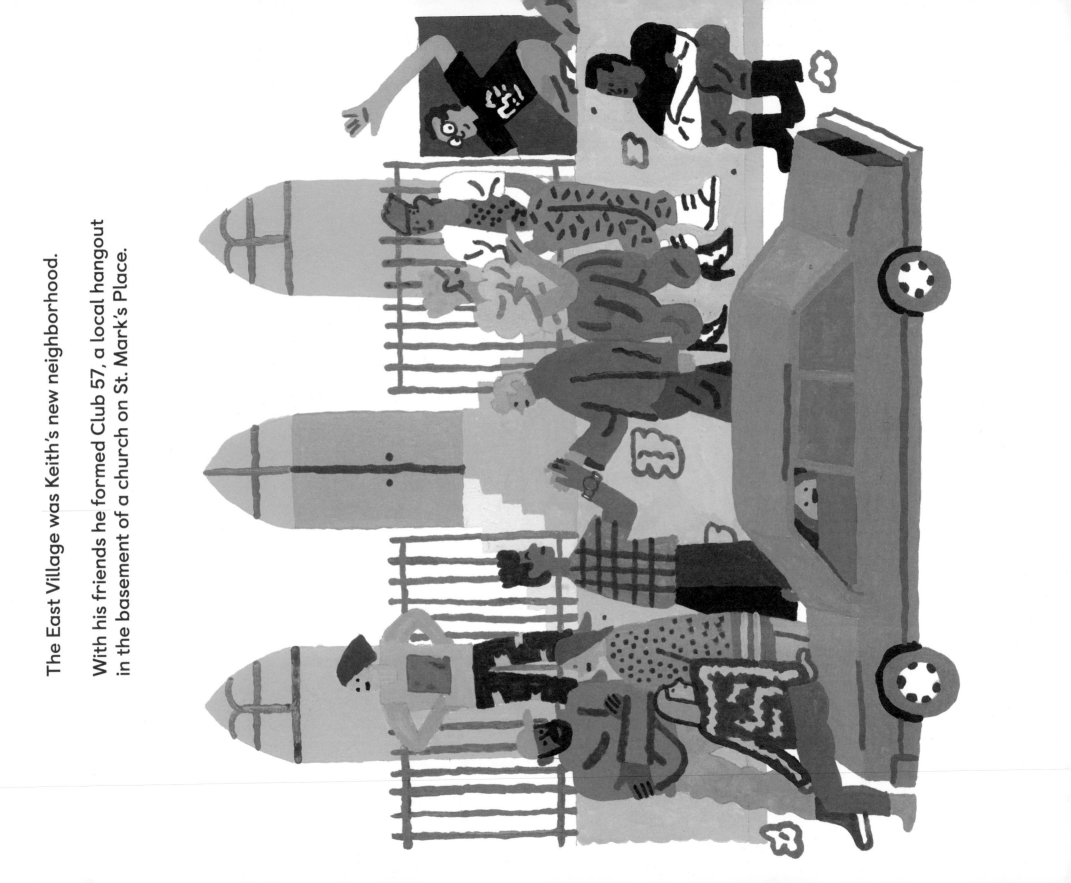

A few years later, when Keith was 23, he fell in love with a deejay named Juan DuBose.

Keith listened to Juan's music while he drew, and Juan cooked big meals in their tiny kitchen.

Together, they were happy.

Keith wasn't earning money from his paintings yet,

so he worked as a bicycle messenger,

a sandwich maker on Seventh Avenue,

a bartender at the Mudd Club,

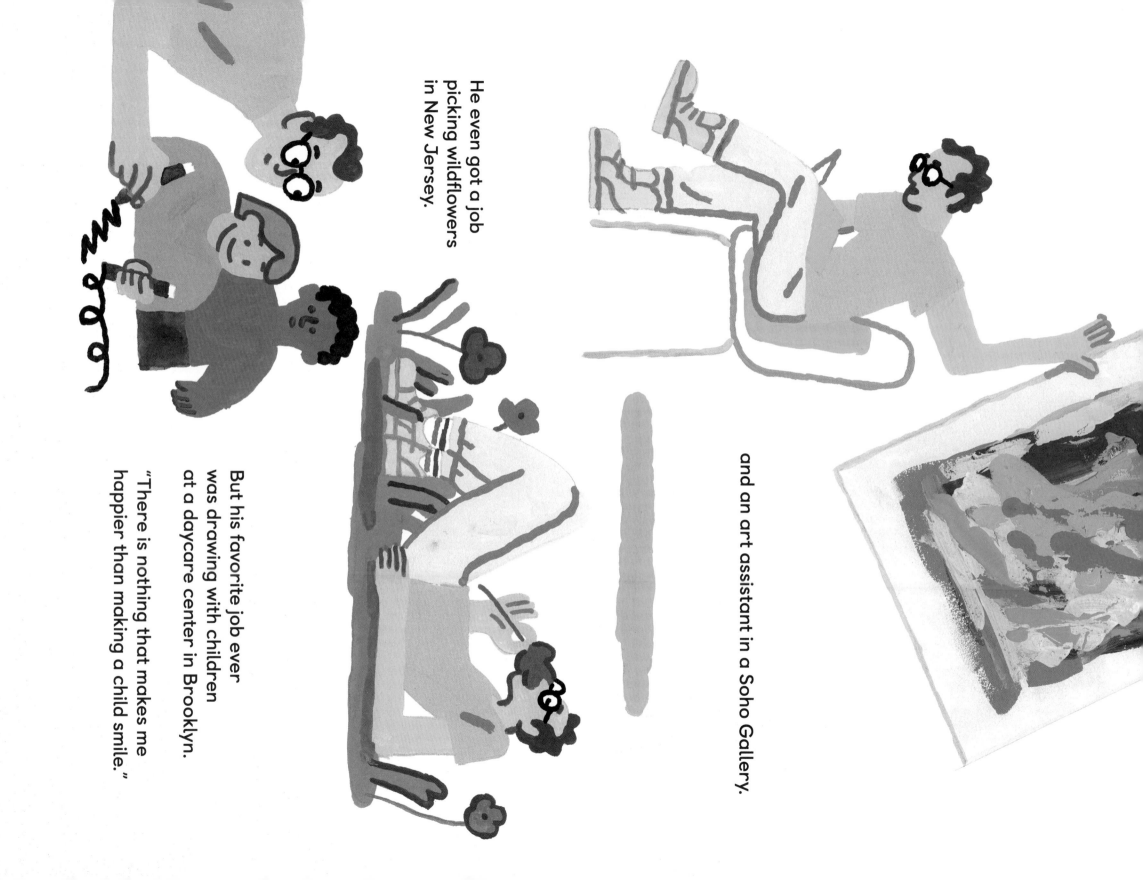

He even got a job picking wildflowers in New Jersey.

and an art assistant in a Soho Gallery.

But his favorite job ever was drawing with children at a daycare center in Brooklyn.

"There is nothing that makes me happier than making a child smile."

With his artist friend Fab 5 Freddy, Keith walked through Alphabet City admiring all of the graffiti.

He loved the colors, the size, the fluid lines, and the blossoming of art on the streets where people could see and enjoy it.

One night, while strolling down King Street in the West Village, Keith heard the thump and beat of music and discovered...

PARADISE +

He was mesmerized by the dancers spinning on their heads and doing the electric boogie as disco and hip-hop rocked the room.

For Keith, drawing and painting were like dancing. He called it "mind-to-hand flow."

DOWNTOWN AND BROOKLYN
←

One day in the subway, Keith noticed blank panels where advertisements used to be.

Suddenly, he zipped up to the street, bought a box of white chalk, dashed back downstairs...

and began drawing on the walls.

People paused as they rushed
from here to there.

For Keith, this was what art
was all about — the moment
when people see it and respond.

Maybe it makes them smile,
maybe it makes them think,
maybe it inspires them to draw
or dance or write or sing.

When Keith was 24, he was offered a major one-man show at the Tony Shafrazi Gallery in Soho.

The opening was packed with artists, musicians, celebrities, and friends, and Keith's family came all the way from Kutztown to celebrate!

Keith's life as an artist was taking off.

But no matter how busy he became or where in the world he went, he always made time for children.

Keith understood kids and they understood him.
There was an unspoken bond between them.

And since children often asked him to draw on their t-shirts, skateboards, and jeans, he always kept a black marker handy.

The kid from Kutztown who had longed to draw on the walls was now receiving invitations to paint murals all over the world.

He was invited to West Germany to paint a stretch of the Berlin Wall, which had been built to divide people, even family and friends, and keep them apart.

Keith believed in the unity of all human beings, so he painted a long chain of interconnected figures.

He also painted a wall with 500 high school students in Chicago, Illinois. It was his longest mural ever at 488 feet, and it took five days to complete.

To honor him, then Mayor Daley declared it "Keith Haring Week."

After watching Keith work, a kid came up to him and said, "I can tell, by the way you paint, that you really love life."

And Keith did love life! Every single day, no matter what difficulties came his way.

Even when he learned that he had a serious illness called AIDS, Keith didn't stop making art and sharing his gifts with the world.

He was overwhelmed by sadness, at first, but then he decided that he would live each day fully, as if it were his last.

"I appreciate everything that has happened, especially the *gift of life* I was given that has created a silent bond between me and children. Children can sense this 'thing' in me."

One morning, while listening to musicians on a New York City street, Keith was recognized in the crowd by a father and son from Italy.

Keith invited them to his studio. In return, they invited him to paint a mural and have an exhibition.

In June 1989, Keith arrived in Pisa to paint a wall on the church of Sant'Antonio. The friars who lived there welcomed him to dinner inside their monastery.

As word spread, people came from all over Europe to meet Keith and watch him work.

A massive crowd waited
for Keith to make his final mark.
When he did, everyone burst
into wild cheering and applause!

The city threw a huge party
with music and dancing in the streets.

Kids, grandparents, soldiers, friars —
everyone celebrated Keith's masterpiece.

"Without question," he said, "Pisa is one
of the highlights of my entire career."

From the time he was four-years-old
drawing with his Dad at the kitchen table,
until the day he died at thirty-one,
Keith remained spontaneous and free,
following his line wherever it would lead.

And though his life ended too soon,
Keith's line is still with us...

...and it goes on forever

BIOGRAPHICAL NOTE

Keith Haring was born on May 4, 1958 in Reading, Pennsylvania. Raised in nearby Kutztown, Keith discovered his love of drawing when he was a kid and dreamed of becoming an artist when he grew up. He graduated from high school in 1976, and after two semesters at the Ivy School of Professional Art in Pittsburgh, Keith moved to New York City. Upon his arrival in 1978, Keith entered into a period of intense creative activity inspired in part by the graffiti that covered the subway cars and spread across walls and storefronts, uptown and down. Fueled by his belief that "art is for everybody," Keith made his first chalk subway drawings in 1980 at the age of 22. In the decade that followed, Keith became one of the most beloved and recognizable artists of his time. He collaborated with other visual artists, dancers, and musicians, including Andy Warhol, William Burroughs, Bill T. Jones, Madonna, Yoko Ono, and Grace Jones. He also committed himself to the fight for social justice, contributing his artwork to causes such as literacy, nuclear disarmament, and AIDS awareness and advocacy. An exuberant creator, Keith traveled all over the world sharing his art, ultimately painting more than 50 public works in hospitals, orphanages, day care centers, and charities. Keith died on February 16, 1990, at the age of 31. His generosity is still felt to this day.

Keith painting a wall at the Palaexpo Museum in Rome, 1984

AUTHOR'S NOTE

I have loved Keith's art since I was fourteen years old. I remember staring at his cover of *A Very Special Christmas* and wondering who "K. Haring" might be. His style immediately drew me in and offered a glimpse of a world beyond my childhood in suburban Southern California. For those of us who grew up before the internet became ubiquitous, a bright fragment from the outer world could feel like an important discovery — and a call.

Eventually, like Keith, I moved to New York City and felt a similar surge of creative inspiration. Then, in 2012, I saw the magnificent Haring retrospective at the Brooklyn Museum. Standing in those galleries, you could feel Keith's energy pulsing through his work like an electric current or a disco tune.

In the gift shop I picked up a copy of the *Journals* and turned to the following passage: "Children know something that most people have forgotten. Children possess a fascination with their everyday existence that is very special and would be very helpful to adults if they could learn to understand and respect it." I had been teaching poetry in NYC public schools for over a decade at this point, and Keith's words rang deep and true.

In the same entry, dated July 7, 1986, Keith wrote: "It is only now that I realize the importance of a biography. I mean I always have realized that I enjoy to read (and have learned many things from) the biographies of artists whom I admire. It is probably my main source of education." Reading this passage, the path appeared before me: to share Keith's story with young readers.

I met some skeptical responses as I began to share the idea, primarily around Keith's homosexuality and illness. Fortunately, my publisher, Claudia Bedrick, and I saw eye-to-eye about the need for greater openness in children's books. What about kids who are dealing with serious illnesses? What about reaching kids who would draw strength and encouragement from Keith's heroic example?

Thirty years ago, Keith was interviewed by *Rolling Stone* for a cover story. It was published in August 1989, just two months after he painted the mural in Pisa and five months before his death. Keith speaks with an arresting sincerity in this interview. When asked whether he would continue to receive invitations to work with kids after publicly revealing his diagnosis of AIDS, Keith expressed doubts but insisted on honesty nonetheless. He was deeply concerned about kids "growing up now":

"It gives so much fuel to the people who are telling you that it's wrong to be who you are. There are so few people who are good openly gay role models or just good people who are respected who are open about their sexuality. Now there has to be openness about all these issues."

While much progress has been made since 1989 — thanks in large part to people like Keith who have dared to be boldly, visibly themselves — there is still a long way to go, especially when discrimination and violence against LGBTQ+ people persist, both at home and around the world.

I wrote this book as an expression of gratitude for Keith's courage and creativity. Since his art may be even more accessible today than it was during his lifetime — you can see his line dancing across t-shirts, posters, skateboards, and walls — what I hope to offer is a glimpse of Keith as a human being. An immensely generous person who held childhood and children at the center of his life, and an extraordinary artist whose spirit still inspires, still delights, still transmits his irrepressible energy of openness, freedom, and joy.

ILLUSTRATOR'S NOTE

My first encounter with Keith Haring was as a student at Art Center College of Design. There is a bright, colorful abstract mural of his painted on the wall right across the hall from the library. I saw this wall almost every single day. Every time I stopped to admire the piece, I would have the same two thoughts: this is the most incredible thing I've ever seen, and how did he make it? The casual fat lines crisscrossing, the vivid washes of color, even the accidental drips are simultaneously effortless and brilliant.

My favorite way to draw is to start in the upper left-hand corner of the page and slowly work my way out. Sometimes I will draw an arm or a cheeseburger too big or too small, and this will affect how I draw the next thing. I'll have to compensate by squeezing something in a tiny space or rendering a bright purple cloud to balance the composition. Drawing as stream-of-consciousness poetry is something that I absorbed in large part from Keith. The way he would approach a wall or a canvas with no hesitation is a constant source of inspiration.

Matthew is a poet, professor, and children's book author. He teaches at Brooklyn College and is a teaching artist in New York City public schools. He is also the author of *Enormous Smallness: A Story of E. E. Cummings*, and *Make Meatballs Sing: The Life & Art of Corita Kent*. He lives with his husband in Brooklyn and Berlin.

Originally from Placentia and Kaohsiung, Josh Cochran is an illustrator and muralist living in Brooklyn. He has received various awards, including a Grammy nomination for album art. An avid traveler and marathon-runner, Josh teaches at the School of Visual Arts, where Keith studied when he first arrived in NYC.

Quotation Sources

Drawing the Line: A Portrait of Keith Haring. Directed by Elisabeth Aubert. New Jersey: Kultur International Films, 1989.

Gruen, John. *Keith Haring: The Authorized Biography*. New York: Prentice Hall Press, 1991.

Haring, Keith. *Journals*. New York: Penguin, 1996.

Henri, Robert. (1923) 2007. *The Art Spirit*. Philadelphia: J.B. Lippincott Company. Reprint, New York: Basic Books.

Off the Wall with Keith and the Kids. Directed by Mike Lorentz. Chicago: PBS, WTTW, 1989.

Sheff, David. *Keith Haring: Just Say Know*. Rolling Stone, August 10, 1989.